Dead Men Tell Tales

Elmer McCurdy: The Strange Tale of the Oklahoma Mummy

John Lindley

Dead Men Tell Tales

© John Lindley

First Edition 2021

Front cover design by Ann Beedham
www.annbeedham.com

Published by Dempsey & Windle
15 Rosetrees
Guildford
Surrey
GU1 2HS
UK
01483 571164
dempseyandwindle.com

British Library Cataloguing-in-Publication Data

ISBN: 978-1-913329-61-7

A catalogue record for this book is available from the British Library

Other collections by John Lindley:

Love & Crossbones (SPM Publications, 2018)
Dylan Thomas: Embers & Sparks (Riverdane, 2014)
Screen Fever (Pinewood Press, 2012)
The Casting Boat (Headland, 2009)
House of Wonders (Riverdane, 2008)
Cheshire Rising (Cheshire County Council, 2005)
Scarecrow Crimes (New Hope International, 2002)
Stills from November Campaigns (Tarantula, 1998)
Cages and Fields (1982)
Pacific Envelope (1976)

Acknowledgements

Nine of the poems in this sequence
originally appeared in the poetry
magazine *Brando's Hat*.

Contents

Introduction

Failed bank and train robber, Elmer McCurdy, did little to distinguish himself in life. Death, however, was a different matter. It was as a corpse that Elmer's career really took off.

Born in Maine in 1880, Elmer McCurdy had been a plumber, miner, soldier and drifter before turning, unsuccessfully, to crime. In March 1911, holding up the Iron Mountain Train, he employed so much nitroglycerin that $4000 in silver coin fused together in the safe and had to be freed with a crowbar by the railway company. Elmer and his four cohorts were left to split a paltry $450. On another occasion, in an attempted bank robbery one night in Kansas, his detonation blew the door of the vault clear across the room but left the interior safe door intact. With the town awakening, the robbers fled, this time with a total take of just $150.

Later that year, Elmer and two others made plans to hold up the Osage payment train which was carrying $400,000. Stopping an earlier mail train by mistake, they made off with only the conductor's watch, a few dollars and some whiskey. Elmer fled north, back to Charlie Revard's ranch where he had been holed up prior to the robbery. He was trailed by a posse and, after hiding out in a barn, drinking whiskey and refusing to surrender, he engaged in an hour long gun battle and was killed. He was 31 years old.

Elmer's body was taken to a funeral parlour in Pawhuska, Oklahoma where it was treated with embalming fluid and arsenic and kept until someone would claim it. Nobody did. He spent five years standing in the corner of the showroom. A figure of fear and fun to the local youngsters, he was even, on occasion, fitted with roller skates and taken outside in play.

On the fifth anniversary of his death, 7th October 1916, his now mummified corpse was claimed by two men posing as relatives, and for many years he became a side show attraction at County Fairs and carnivals across small town America. Passing from owner to owner, Elmer had, by now, become the property of Louis Sonney of the Sonney Amusement Company. With Sonney's excursion into the Exploitation Film business, the mummy became a convenient prop in cinema lobbies, imaginatively employed as the victim of illicit sex, drugs or whatever moral evil the particular film showing portrayed.

In the late 50s, Don Sonney inherited his father's business and Elmer's body was stored in a casket and used as nothing more than a gag for those who both worked there and visited. Two decades later, the body was sold to the owner of the Hollywood Wax Museum who in turn quickly donated him, unused, to friends who ran a side show at Long Beach, California. When they moved on they left the unidentified body, assumed to be a dummy, and it was daubed with iridescent paint and hung by a noose, naked and anonymous, in the 'Laff in the Dark' ghost train ride.

On 7th December 1976, Universal Television, filming an episode of the series 'The Six Million Dollar Man' on that site, came across the hanged figure, recognised it as human and informed the authorities. A coin and a torn entrance ticket to 'Sonney's' was found in the mouth of the mummy. From the starting point of this clue, the body's history and identity was eventually traced. Elmer was flown back to Oklahoma and, on the 22nd April 1977, buried with dignity at the bottom of the cemetery's hill where other criminals and outcasts resided. Before the grave was filled in, six feet of concrete was poured on top of the coffin to ensure that Elmer McCurdy could at last rest in peace.

Rope Trick

7th December 1976, The Pike, Long Beach, California

Well, it's some kind of story's starting point perhaps
but the Six Million Dollar Man is not the story.
The Six Million Dollar Man is not the main man.
Lee Majors has no role, not even a minor one.
The hero, if there is one, and there isn't,
will be played by a runty vagabond,
a near half foot shorter than the Bionic Man
and withered into something even less
for his last comeback scene.

It's him we've come to see: make-up intact,
making his infrared impact
and more naked than even nature intended.
He pirouettes for us if we touch him
and of course we do. He asks for it.
This is his latest trick; this rope trick.

Come. Gently but firmly nudge his good arm
and take him for a spin. Don't be a killjoy.
When the braided threads
above the noose's knot braid yet more
before they untwist and hang still,
you'll have a changed view.
You can't say this figure isn't fun
whichever way you look at it.

John Doe #255

December 1976, Autopsy Lab, Los Angeles Coroner's Office

First the features then the name.
These are the bookends of the stations of death's cross,
the outreaching degrees of disappearance.
(Photographs may survive.)
From unclaimed to unidentified
his has been a specifics-shedding process
that's spanned six decades of not resting in peace.

John Doe number 255 settles on a slab
and when all supposition fails,
when all of the guesswork has been guessed
he lets his tale spin unvarnished
from a cracked mandible and jaw
the moment it's unhinged from his head.

Cough up, John Doe.
You who once coughed up
the phlegm of zinc from an ore mine,
cough up and tell us about yourself.
Here's a 1924 corrosion-coloured coin
and a sheath of ticket stubs.
Here begins the geography.
From here we piece the biography.

It's not much but it's a start.
He reminds us of the reminders
we may leave at the end
if that leaving leaves no family or friend,
no card or forwarding address,
just teeth, a tattoo or two, the indent of a ring;
less than *he* gives us to go on.

"Go on", he says. "Go on."
We take the few clues from his unburied corpse
and begin to dig.

The Day of the Dead
December 1976, Autopsy Lab, Los Angeles Coroner's Office

No *calavera* this.
No sugar skull for a single day.
This one stays sheathed in the slenderest of skins,
a thin tissue of icing browning the brow.

No *Dia de Muertos* this.
Every day's a dead day for him,
though he lives each and every one of them
above ground, bound in a bandage of petrified skin.

No *calavera* this.
This is the real thing. The genuine article.
Whilst no lettered name appears on his forehead,
this is the real McCoy. The real McCurdy.

Mug Shots

29th November 1910. Buchanan County Jail, St. Joseph, Missouri.

Two prints, but the postcards put them together:
profile and full face. I like best those sequenced
to show a good looking Elmer McCurdy
having a good look at himself in his military uniform.
His shoulders, banded by the braces of his overalls,
are pushed back and his expression is as semi-sad
as you'd expect the semi-guilty to be.

He's soon out of there, triggered by his own creative plea
of innocence, with less than a bad nine months to live.
For all the grotesques to follow, he leaves these
two age-smattered exposures as the only shots of him alive.
Dying from the inside before dying from the out
he has less time to age than they did.
He gets there in the end (whenever you count the end),
wrinkling back to his bones, everyone
then no-one to look. Not even him.

The Ballad of the Oklahoma Outlaw

Come and gather round, you people
 For the tale I'll tell is true
'Bout a penny-ante outlaw
 And the things he tried to do

Known as Davidson or Davis
 And lots of other names
Each and all Elmer McCurdy
 Who'd been born and raised in Maine

Was a plumber and a miner
 And a soldier in his time
But when he got out of the army
 He turned his hand to crime

A drifter and a drinker
 With some felons at his side
He failed to blow a train's safe
 No matter how he tried

So he packed in more explosives
 And that safe blew open wide
Left four thousand silver dollars
 Melted to its sides

At The Citizens Bank in Kansas
  He used nitroglycerin but
He blew the bank to kingdom come
  And the vault remained tight shut

But Elmer and two buddies
  Thought they'd chance their arm again
At four hundred thousand dollars
  Riding on the Katy Train

Near Okesa, Oklahoma
  They forced the train to brake
Boarded it and found they'd stopped
  The wrong train by mistake

The three of them took to the hills
  Then went their separate ways
And a posse tracked them through the rain
  By the hoof prints in the clay

Elmer hid at Charlie Revard's ranch
  With whiskey and a gun
And both he and it were loaded
  When he heard the sheriff come

He wouldn't go without a fight
  Though the odds were 4 to 1
But a bullet put an end to it
  And Elmer's race was run

They put him in a wagon
  And they hauled him into town
You can kill Elmer McCurdy
  But can you keep him down?

So farewell to all you people
  My story's almost done
But Elmer's isn't over, no
  It's only just begun.

Wanted

Round these parts,
when the unwanted suddenly become 'Wanted',
it comes down to degrees of notoriety
whether it's 'Dead or Alive.'
It's an out of reach status for Elmer with
'one of the smallest hauls in the history of train robbery'
on his slim CV of crime. It doesn't help to flesh
out the detail, the thin inventory:
a pocket watch and coat, jugs of beer, a revolver,
small change and two demijohns of whiskey.
Captured he's worth two thousand bucks,
dead he's worth nothing.
At least that's what you'd think
but when Elmer goes down
irony comes out shooting.

Cornered – Shoot-out at Charlie's
Osage Hills, Oklahoma

Elmer wasn't given to reflection
but holed up at Charlie's between the Candy River
and the Kansas Line
he thought about the wrong train
after months of thinking about the right one.
He thought about the conductor's watch
and the whiskey and then about the right train
with its riches untouched.
And he thought about explosives and another train
where he'd packed so much nitro
he'd seen his future melt before his eyes.
And he reflected on a splintery bank
going off like an alarm
and on his soldiering and mining for ore.
And now he was plumbing and schooling
and howling for milk
and all the time he was going back
there were men with guns and intent coming forward
beyond the barn's warm womb.
And Elmer liquored up,
grew up, stood up,
took the last, the very last hit
from a bottle of rye
and went and got killed.

And Nothing but the Truth

Now, stop me if you've heard this one but
there was this Irishman who wasn't Irish,
born in both Washington and Bangor on the same day.

Well, the way it was told to me was
he became a plumber, fireman and miner
who never did a day's work in his life
and who joined the army then deserted
with an honourable discharge.

And have you heard about Davis, Curtis and Amos?
Well, seems no-one could tell them apart,
not even the father who wasn't around
or the aunt who was really the mother and who was dead
so they all became a kind of one-man gang called
Elmer McCurdy or McCready or McCarty or something.

Or maybe the one about
the most notorious outlaw in the West.
The one no-one's ever heard of.

Or how about this one? A man walks into a barn
and orders whiskey, gets some, drinks it
and when the posse arrive he's so drunk that when he fires his gun
he finds he couldn't hit the side of a ... well, barn.

But the best bit is the end.
Seems he was shot in his sleep whilst stood up and shooting,
taking a single slug through his head and his chest.

Drew his last breath in a field and in a barn,
dying in the long arms of the law who stood 300 yards from him
at the time, immediately after he'd drunk poison,
shot down his throat via a 32-20 calibre bullet.

That last bit occurred in 1911.
The 7th and 8th October, to be precise.
Check the newspapers, eyewitnesses and historians,
you just see if I'm not telling you the truth.
I tell you, feller, you couldn't make it up.

Pretty Boy Floyd – Lies and the Nature of Coincidence

"This is the West, sir. When the legend becomes fact, print the legend." — 'The Man Who Shot Liberty Valance'. (1962) Directed by John Ford.

The year Floyd checked into Oklahoma
was the very same year Elmer checked out –
as far as living goes. Floyd came from a
dirt-poor background, of that there is no doubt,
but many of his 'facts', like McCurdy's,
are as fluid and long lasting as em-
balming oil could prove to be. We heard his
story twisted so much in requiem
that it might as well have been Robin Hood
moving in to replace Elmer's Jesse James
if you wanted the myths. The facts are good
too, parallels of same or nearly the same:
the same month, October, saw both men die –
30 and 31 years old. No lie.

A Time of Dying

An 'out of wedlock' birth,
an 'out of luck' life
and an 'out of time' death;
not a 'run out of time' death
(we all do a 'run out of time' death)
more a 'dead before his time' death.

What time would that be exactly?
What *was* Elmer's time?
Beyond his 31 living conscious years
when would the dying time have come?
What would the click-over calendar tiles record
if not OCT 7 1911? Who knows?
We don't and *he* sure as hell didn't.

They always speak of one's time, don't they?
Whoever 'they' are – the songwriters, perhaps,
with their plaintive *When my time has come*.
Maybe Elmer's never truly did.
Maybe he slept through his
and chose to lay low for a while
before finding his feet, moving on, spending years
having the time of his death.

Drying Out

Johnson Funeral Home, Pawhuska, Oklahoma

Don't mind him – he don't bite.
Still as a pause,
a cocktail of arsenic and air
propped against the wall,
downcast eyes arrowed along
the barrel of a pinched nose.

Elmer dries out,
holds a semblance of himself,
turns brown as old sellotape
but hangs together,
projects the taut links of his spine
but doesn't let them through,
keeps his bones housed
and hinted at.

He has feet like Jesus
think the kids.
They picture them punctured,
a fence post nail
driven in to the hilt

but not when shod with skates,
wheeled out amidst laughter
into the dangerous sun,
his tinderbox heart not in it.

Roll Up

Death rolls on.
Down here the air smacks of snake oil.
Dave and Davinia, twinned at the hip,
crabwalk from tent to tent
in a free show just once
but everything else costs money.

There's always another sideshow
and always another side –
some dupe, some con in the 10 in 1:
a grotto where a bored mermaid,
slicked in fins,
swims the dry Mississippi air;
a lair where women sport beards
with the texture of hemp;
an inner sanctum of hydra-headed babies
and midgets on stilts
and *It's only a buck, just one slim dollar*
for the 'Mysteries of the Universe'.

Elmer goes where he's told,
sleeps awake with the props in a trailer,
comes out at showtime.
And he's never been so decorated:
bank heists and stick-ups
and twenty-six slayings to his name.

He turns legend for the day
on a rich litany of lies.
People gawp in belief.
A toffee apple sun sets
in a cotton candy sky.
The ferris wheel ticks to its conclusion.
The carnival pulls pegs,
drops canvas, loads trucks.
Across America mummies move out.
Death rolls on.

Exploitation

He catches on like syphilis
and all of the 'bally'* boils down to *Catch this film today –*
tomorrow there'll be nothing but Law in its place.

Just as Elmer, tricked up and erect in the lobby,
is 3-dimensional, as far as the celluloid nudes go
we punters can only wish for as much.

Still, their pre-advertised madness is in hammy evidence.
Whether from reefers, the Devil or sex
we must try and put their acting down to that.

In contrast, though as stiff as the actors,
Elmer plays his part with aplomb
or at least something akin to plomb.

But for on his face he has no lines, no speaking part
but his silence speaks – if not volumes –
a deeply forbidding sentence or two.

It is easily translatable: *Folks, live clean,*
don't go to the places I have been
or see the things that I have seen.

Dollars at the door don't buy the promised thrills
but they do buy us *that* stark lesson:
Stay away. Never make this mistake again.

Elmer has no choice but to make it. Again and again
and again and again and again and again
and again and again and again.

*ballyhoo

Grindhouse (Song)

Gotta get down to the Grindhouse
Doesn't matter what they show
Child Bride or *Reefer Madness*
She Freak or *Gambling with Souls*
Gotta get there in a hurry
Park my car just off the Strip
Swagger in at weekend with my tongue in my cheek and
My wallet riding on my hip

It has to be a B Picture
Has to be trashy and cheap
With plenty of shocks and plenty of blood
And in a theatre that's filled with creeps
Let the movie be hot with the kind of plot
That an ape could understand
Give it so much sex and so many x's
That they're bound to try and get it banned

B Picture. Be a B Picture
B Picture. Be a B Picture
B Picture. Be a B Picture
Yeah

There's some joker standing just inside –
A gross-out from his head to his toe
They've got him tricked out in a costume of rags
And they've stuck him there as part of the show
I guess he's meant as some kinda warning
Of what your sins can lead you to be
Well, whether his rap is the weed or the clap
It sure won't happen to me

A real low budget picture
That's about as high as I want it
With plenty of flesh and plenty of thrills
And something freaky in the lobby to front it
Wanna show my girlfriend that he don't scare me
Stick my ticket stub between his teeth
He looks like a dummy or some kinda mummy
Though my girl swore she heard him breathe

Low budget. Low, low budget.
Low budget. Low, low budget.
Low budget. Low, low budget.
Yeah

Ex-ploi-tation. Sex-ploi-tation
Ex-ploi-tation. Sex-ploi-tation
Ex-ploi-tation. Sex-ploi-tation
Yeah

One time down at the Grindhouse
I swear I saw my priest slip in
Had a hat pulled down across his eyes
And his collar up to his chin
You never know who you'll meet there
(Well, that's not strictly true)
There's one sad excuse for a victim they use
Who you know is gonna be on view

Today they're showing *Slaves in Bondage*
Sex Madness coming around
Hope they get time for *Brand of Shame*
Before the cops come and close 'em down
I wanna see *Panties Inferno*
Two Thousand Maniacs! too
Get in line behind the dead man inside
And form a disorderly queue

B Picture. Be a B Picture
B Picture. Be a B Picture
B Picture. Be a B Picture
Yeah

Exhibit 'A'

Pride of place –
rigid by the booth,
each new movie trailered in his given past.
Alternately dead from too much dope,
too much sex, too much life;
counterfeit wife a widow to the weed,
fantasy kids orphaned by drink.
He's scapegoat, leper and portent,
the destiny of the depraved;
one of those scorched examples of God's vengeance
who explode from Hell's furnace
to Hell's Kitchen and beyond.
He speaks in a language he'd not recognise
with a voice he never owned
of a past he never had;
his crimes writ large
on a card around his neck.
It can't go on. Under the masks
the real Elmer McCurdy
must stand up and be counted.
Besides, he *can't* stay –
there's a train in an arcade at Long Beach
he'll always be in time for.

Cold Storage
'Exploitation Row', Cordova St., L.A.

No hurry.
At *Sonney's* Death keeps office hours.
Elmer's underused
but it's then that he's needed
when he's needed at all.
It's not a difficult job
to be yourself or what you've become
for the purpose of fun or fright;
to be thick-skinned when in truth
your skin is a wafer of Autumn;
to shed an arm for a laugh
and have it black taped back.
In time though
all the jokes are out at the elbows
and the Oklahoma Outlaw's
just so much clutter, so much space.
It's then that it's time to move on,
to be fairground bound
where the *Laff in the Dark*
is as hollow as he is.

Laff in the Dark
The Pike, Long Beach, California

The Laff in the Dark. The Laff in the Dark.
Hold onto your sides. It's a helluva lark
when the cars lurch forward with a clang and a spark
down at the Nu-Pike Amusement Park.

You can do what you like, do what you like
if your girlfriend permits it down at the Pike
but watch out for those coffins and masks and the like,
take care that the ghouls and the goblins don't strike.

Turn out the lights. Turn out the lights.
Turn on the music and turn up the frights.
Her skirt is real short and her sweater real tight.
This is a dark ride of many delights.

Look out here he comes! Look out here he comes!
Her screams drown the noise of the rails as they hum
whilst Elmer just hangs there, that son of a gun,
not even a hint of some proud martyrdom.

Look out here he comes! Look out there he goes!
The mummified figure without any clothes,
a shrivelled up spectre that hangs there and glows,
a dirt cheap example of death's rich tableaux,
one more of the Fun House's naff cameos,
not real convincing, but okay, I suppose.

This is a Dark Ride   (Song)

Do you wanna talk about that tipping point
When life tips into death?
Wanna talk about that split-second slice
When breath becomes no breath?
Or do you wanna distance your mind
From the figure with the scythe who lurks behind?
Wanna run away and hide?
This is a dark ride

We ride these narrow silver rails
We feel those switchback curves
We see ghosts and ghouls and witches and things
But it doesn't shred our nerves
We know how to play. We know the game
You pay for your ticket and you board this train
But though your eyes are open wide
This is a dark ride

A few minutes in with your hand on her thigh
And the Ghost Train plays its ace
The body of a man swings naked and red
And you meet him face to face
Your girlfriend buries her head in the thick of your scarf
She stifles a scream and you let out a laugh
You gotta think about your pride
This is a dark ride

Better get in line. Better get in line
Count up your nickels and cents and dimes
Weigh the cost of the con with the use of your time
You wanna know what's inside

You think it's cool that for the price of a buck
You can smile in the face of death
It's nothing more to you than a *Laff in the Dark*
With a girl around your neck
You figure that it's all kicks and fun
But what you don't get is not everyone
Gets out of here alive
This is a dark ride

Ghost Train – Elmer Speaks!

The Pike, Long Beach, California

There's a sense of belonging
whatever your place
if you've been there for more than a moment
and I've been here for moments untold
with a horse hair necktie
and a fool's gold glow,
watching the cars from out
of my left eye, right eye, left.
I've heard the two seaters
rattle the curves like Winchesters reloading.
I've seen lips together,
hands in blouses, in the dark of the car
and in a young girl's skirt
and, swaying in the dark,
it don't do nothing to me.
I keep a paper skinned hand
over my shrivelled cock
but nothing's stirring.
I'm in a place that reads through
lipstick and paint and skin and all
to the scaffold of life itself
and if I had one good hand to raise
I'd raise it now and say STOP.
Take one good look.
Don't I scare you half to death?

Mirrors and smoke they'd say.
A pity. Half dead
they'd meet me halfway.

Numbers Game

7 days (with rest) to create the world.
1 lucky shot to leave it.
'Lucky for some' as they say.
Elmer died on the 7th,
had his remains stolen on the 7th
and turned up, decades on, hanging from a noose on the 7th.
If there are indeed 7 heavens
as the *Torah* and the *Quran* maintain,
then Elmer never made it through the gate of any of them.
It's perhaps a number too sacred for the likes of him,
him being, after all, one of life's bad guys.
But 'lucky'? No, I don't think you could say lucky.
Not Elmer. Not in birth, death or after-death.
Maybe he got 1 more roll of the dice
than the rest of us get, carrying on as he did
when he should have been done. Didn't count.
No matter how many rolls of the dice you gave Elmer
I don't think his number would have ever come up.
Not one that he wanted.

Homecoming – Elmer's Last Ride

22nd April 1977, Summit View Cemetery, Guthrie,
Oklahoma

Elmer has his ticket
and if his dry bone hands can't hold it
his thin-lipped mouth can.
And it's a ticket home
to a home of sorts.
Its torn tongue tells tales
of *Sonney's*, of recognition,
of reclamation and rest.
And he's balsa wood light
when they take him,
red as a beet, to Guthrie.
And he's lowered into a company of thieves
and they'd know him anywhere,
dressed for the occasion
in his last life's skin
and this morning's new hair.

Graveside

Damn me if he don't find a way out of there,
you just see if he don't.
That sonofabitch wouldn't stay put
with half an arsenal of lead in him
so half a ton of concrete on his fine pine box
won't hold him. No. He's seen too much of life
since dying: rode the rails, cruised the highways,
skated alongside himself in store front windows.
He's tasted the sweet free moving air
through an open door; held the mucus of machine oil
in his hollow nostrils when the ghost train reeks by;
kept stiff as a stiff in autos that bounced
each new surrogate parent like popcorn in a pan;
seen a two-headed stag and a human crab.
I swear, if nobody comes for Elmer
he'll be coming for them, you betcha,
bad arm under the other,
coin clutched under his fig of a tongue
to buy booze.

Lullaby

Dust's on the prairie, a buzzard's on high,
A ghost train tornado is rumbling by.
Everything's moving but one thing is clear –
Elmer McCurdy is staying right here.

Tumbleweeds tumble, prairie dogs cry,
There's a knock on his tombstone, a crack in the sky
And a Lazarus wind tosses questions around
But Elmer McCurdy stays deaf underground.

Though townsfolk up sticks and go scurrying by
He's six feet under – let sleeping dogs lie.
Hush! Hush! Whisper who dares!
Elmer McCurdy is going nowheres.

John Lindley is a freelance poet, songwriter and creative writing tutor. An experienced performer, he has read at Ledbury Poetry Festival and at numerous other festivals around the UK. He runs workshops for writers' groups, and in prisons, schools, universities, day care centres and for those with learning difficulties. Widely published and a prizewinner in a number of international competitions, his poetry has also been broadcast on radio. His tenth and prizewinning collection of poetry, *Love & Crossbones*, was published in 2018. A second album of his songs, *Trickery, Thieves & Luck* was released in October 2020. He also performs his own songs in the band *John Lindley & the Poachers* for the benefit of various charities.

www.johnflindley.wordpress.com